ALSO BY ZEINA HASHEM BECK

**POETRY COLLECTIONS**
*Louder than Hearts* (2017)
*To Live in Autumn* (2014)

**CHAPBOOKS**
*3arabi Song* (2016)
*There Was and How Much There Was* (2016)

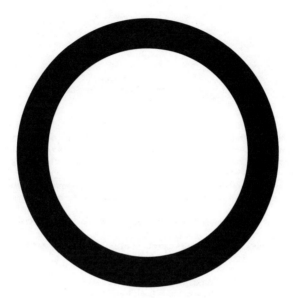

# ZEINA HASHEM BECK

PENGUIN POETS

PENGUIN BOOKS
An imprint of Penguin Random House LLC
penguinrandomhouse.com

"A Note on O" by Asmaa Azaizeh. Printed by permission of Asmaa Azaizeh.

LIBRARY OF CONGRESS CATALOGING-IN-PUBLICATION DATA
Names: Hashem Beck, Zeina, author.
Title: O / Zeina Hashem Beck.
Description: [New York] : Penguin Books, [2022] | Series: Penguin poets |
Some poems in English and Arabic.
Identifiers: LCCN 2021050079 (print) | LCCN 2021050080 (ebook) |
ISBN 9780143136897 (paperback) | ISBN 9780525508373 (ebook)
Subjects: LCGFT: Poetry.
Classification: LCC PR9570.L43 H376 2022 (print) |
LCC PR9570.L43 (ebook) | DDC 821/.92—dc23/eng/20211103
LC record available at https://lccn.loc.gov/2021050079
LC ebook record available at https://lccn.loc.gov/2021050080

Printed in the United States of America
1st Printing

Set in More Pro
Designed by Sabrina Bowers

# Acknowledgments

Thank you to the editors of these publications, in which the following poems, sometimes in earlier versions, first appeared:

*Academy of American Poets Poem-a-Day series*: "There, There, Grieving," "Time,"

*The Adroit Journal*: "Ghazal: Hands," "Dear white critic, رفيقي في الرحيل،"

*The Atlantic*: "The Body Fails in a Foreign City"

*The Common*: "Sometimes All You Can Do Is Wait"

*Cordite Poetry Review*: "Ode to My Husband, Who Brings the Music"

*Discontent*: "Pilgrim"

*Iron Horse Literary Review*: "Fools Rush In," "Say it,"

*The Lifted Brow*: "daily كلّ يوم," "prophecy نبوّة"

*MIT Technology Review*: "Thank You, Antidepressants"

*Modern Poetry in Translation*: "Ode to Leaving غربة"

*Mom Egg Review*: "triptych: voice"

*Nashville Review*: "Immortality (or on turning 36)"

*New England Review*: "Bulbul"

*Ploughshares*: "ode to the afternoon"

*Poetry*: "Ghazal: With Prayer," "Souk," "Poem Beginning & Ending with My Birth"

*Poetry International*: "UNBREAKABLE" (and a reprint of "Ghazal: Hands")

*Poetry London*: "triptych: you & my country & i"

*Raleigh Review*: "Ode to Lipstick"

*Redivider*: "Everything Here Is an Absolute"

*The Scores*: "Morning Prayer"

*Southeast Review*: "Heirloom," "Flamingos"

*Triquarterly*: "Ode to Babel نشيد الانتظار," "Ode to Disappointment"

*wildness*: "triptych: reprise," "What the Returning Do"

"blue أزرق" appeared in the anthology *And We Chose Everything* (Turning Point Books, 2018). "Say Love Say God" appeared in the chapbook *There Was and How Much There Was* (Smith|Doorstop, 2016). "Ode to Disappointment" was reprinted in the anthology *The Long Devotion: Poets Writing Motherhood* (University of Georgia Press, 2022). "Ghazal: In this City" was commissioned by Warehouse421 for an exhibition titled *The Architecture of Loneliness*.

Sincere thanks to the presses and journals that published my work. Deepest gratitude to the Penguin Books team: Paul Slovak and Allie Merola for believing in *O* and for your moving words; Lauren Peters-Collaer for the gorgeous book cover; Brian Tart, Patrick Nolan, Andrea Schulz, Norina Frabotta, Gabriel Levinson, Anne McPeak, Nick Sturm, Mahmoud Hosny, Sabrina Bowers for your indispensable help ushering *O* into the world.

Thank you, Naomi Shihab Nye, for your light and support.

Thank you, friends who've made Beirut home and listened as I rambled about poetry and life: Huda Fakhreddine, Lina Abyad, Sahar Assaf, and Rami Elnakat.

Thank you, friends who've made Dubai home and listened as I rambled about poetry and life: Leila Ghandour, Hind Shoufani, Farah Chamma, Hani Yakan, Nada Kaissi, Lina El-Zein, Frank Dullaghan, Rewa Zeinati, Hajer Mosleh, Danabelle Gutierrez, Farah Ali, Rasha Alduwaisan, Samar Abdeljaber, Maan Jalal, and Michelle Abboud.

Thank you to the community of writers and poets who hold and uplift: Hala Alyan, Lina Mounzer, Zahra Hankir, Kaveh Akbar, Paige Lewis, Tiana Clark, Leila Chatti, Fady Joudah, Deema Shehabi, Lena Tuffaha Khalaf, Safia Elhillo, Asmaa Azaizeh, Golan Haji, Marilyn Hacker, Karthika Nair, Marcia Lynx Qualey, Saleem Haddad, Noor Naga, Tishani Doshi, Joey Ayoub, Nasri Atallah, George Abraham, Raymond Antrobus, Anthony Anaxagorou, Lisa Luxx, and many others.

Thank you to my childhood friend and sister Rana Kamareddine.

Mama, thank you for the confidence and validation and fire.

Baba and my brothers, I love you, thank you.

Amto Yathreb, thank you for the sparkle.

Marwan, partner and childhood sweetheart, thank you for your unwavering love and support.

My husband's family that's become mine, thank you.

Leina, my beautiful firstborn, thank you for the laughter and the warmest hugs.

Thank you, Aya, my hero with the scintillating eyes and biggest heart.

Thank you, reader, for spending time with these poems.

# Note on the Bilingual Poems, the Duets

The idea of the Duet is that the poems in English and Arabic exist separately and in relationship to each other. The English lines are a poem in English, and the same goes for the Arabic lines. Both languages should also form a poem when read together. When the Arabic and English appear within the same stanza, this means the lines are some sort of translation or echo of one another (sometimes the echo is a contradiction).

# كلمة عن O من أسماء عزايزة، مؤلِّفة "لا تصدقوني إن حدثتكم عن الحرب"

ليس للشعر لسان جاهز، كما يقول الشاعر أنسي الحاج. وليس لدى زينة لغة أو معانٍ جاهزة. هذه الشاعرة تسعى في البحث عن معنى مثل من يسري ليلاً، في غفلةٍ منّا، نحو عوالمَ موازية ومجهولة. ذلك لأن شعرها بارع في التحطيم، وقد أقول في تحطيم معابدها هي، وبارع في محاولة تصوير اللا مرئي منها. كل شيء قابل للتفكك والانعتاق من هذه المعابد؛ الوطن، الحب، الحنين، المدينة، العائلة، التاريخ الشخصي. حتّى القصيدة تنعتق في كثير من الأحيان من شكلها، مرّة تختبر السرد وأخرى تختبر الاقتصاد والتكثيف. هذا الانعتاق الصريح والمتكرر من الموضوع والشكل هو ثمرة الكتابة الحرّة.

نقرأ في «O» قصيدة حرّة حتى من تاريخ الشاعرة الشخصيّ. فبقدر ما تخلص له زينة عاطفيًّا، بقدر ما تحوّره وتعجنه بيدها وتشكّله على مزاجها كي تنجو من قسوته. هكذا، تقترح هذه المجموعة كتابة بديعة للذاكرة. فالذاكرة في هذه المجموعة مادة خاضعة للتخييل والتأويل. عبر صور ساحرة، تضيف زينة على الماضي طبقات من الزمن والمسافة، ثم سرعان ما تهشّمها بنفسها، فلا تأبه بالخسائر التي تُحدثها هذه المواجهات الحادّة. سننظر إلى أنفسنا في المرآة ونعترف بأنّنا أوّل هذه الخسائر، وأنّنا أكثر الأشياء تحوّلاً في ذاكرتنا.

قراءة هذه المجموعة تشبه السير على حواف الأشياء. لا الوطن وطن تمامًا، لا الحبّ حبّ تمامًا، لا المنفى منفى تمامًا. حتّى اللغة ليست مكانًا آمنًا. «كلّ اللغات تُربكني»، تقول زينة. سيشعر القارئ بغربة فظيعة مع أفكارها الناجزة عن الأشياء، لكن بانتماء مدهش للعالم الذي تبنيه زينة. وهو عالم مشيّد من حيوات تعتّمت وذكريات فلتت من بين أصابعنا وشخوص غائبة، لكن مع ذلك، نبدو كأنّنا دُسنا لتونا عالمًا جديدًا لم يُعش. الشعر وحده قادر على تعويضنا عن فداحة أن يهجرنا كلّ شيء. وقراءة «O» تذكّرنا كم نحن بأمسّ الحاجة إلى الشعر.

# A Note on *O* from Asmaa Azaizeh, author of *Don't Believe Me If I Talk to You of War*

"There is no set language for poetry," as Lebanese poet Ounsi el-Hajj says. And there's no set language or ready meanings for Zeina. This poet is on the search for meaning as one who wanders at night, without us expecting it, toward parallel and unknown worlds. This is because her poetry is skillful at trying to portray the unseen; it is skillful at destruction—and, I want to say, the destruction of her own temples. Everything can fall apart and be liberated from these temples: homeland, love, longing, city, family, and personal history. Even the poem, at times narrative and at times economical and condensed, is often liberated from its form. This honest and persistent emancipation from form and content is the fruit of free writing.

In *O*, we read poetry that is free even from the poet's personal history. For as much as Zeina is emotionally faithful, she transforms and kneads her personal history, shaping it at her whim in order to escape its cruelty. This is how this collection astoundingly captures memory in writing; in this book, memory is open for imagination and interpretation. With captivating images, Zeina adds layers of time and distance to the past, then hurries to shatter them without caring about the losses that result from these brutal confrontations. We will look at ourselves in the mirror and admit we are the first losses, and we are the most changeable things in our memory.

Reading this collection is like walking on the edge of things. Neither home is fully home, nor love is fully love, nor exile is fully exile. Even language isn't a safe place: "all languages confuse me," Zeina writes. Readers will feel estranged from their received ideas about things, all the while wondrously belonging to the world that Zeina creates—a world of obscured lives, absent people, and memories that slip from our fingers, but a world that nevertheless feels new, unlived. Only poetry is capable of making up for the fact that everything deserts us, and reading *O* reminds us how urgently we need poetry.

# Contents

Ghazal: With Prayer ○ *1*

# 1

There, There, Grieving ○ *5*

ode to the afternoon ○ *7*

Ghazal: Hands ○ *9*

Pilgrim ○ *10*

daily كلّ يوم ○ *11*

triptych: you & my country & i ○ *14*

Dear white critic, رفيقي في الرحيل، ○ *15*

Everything Here Is an Absolute ○ *18*

Revolution Song ○ *19*

ode to fear of ○ *21*

# 2

Poem Beginning & Ending with My Birth ○ *25*

Bulbul ○ *31*

blue أزرق ○ *33*

What the Returning Do ○ *36*

Heirloom ○ *37*

Every Soul Needs Windows ○ *38*

Ghazal: My Daughter ○ *40*

Flamingos ○ *41*

Time, ○ *43*

# 3

Conversation with Sun God ○ *47*

prophecy نبوّة ○ *48*

Ghazal-Ode for My Body ○ *49*

Say it, ○ *52*

triptych: voice ○ *53*

Souk ○ *54*

Incredible ○ *56*

Ode to Lipstick ○ *57*

Sometimes All You Can Do Is Wait ○ *59*

Ode to Leaving غربة ○ *61*

We Are Young We Are Beautiful ○ *65*

UNBREAKABLE ○ *67*

The Body Fails in a Foreign City ○ *69*

# 4

Fools Rush In ○ *73*

Say Love Say God ○ *74*

Ode to My Husband, Who Brings the Music ○ *76*

when we are we are ○ *78*

Ode to Babel نشيد الانتظار ○ *79*

triptych: reprise ○ *82*

Ghazal: In this City ○ *83*

Ode to Disappointment ○ *84*

Things My Daughters Said ○ *86*

Immortality (or on turning 36) ○ *87*

Ode to Hunger ○ *89*

Ghazal: Dear Beirut ○ *90*

Thank You, Antidepressants ○ *91*

Morning Prayer ○ *93*

# Ghazal: With Prayer

The herons were no longer safe in the sky. They flew with prayer,
then fell to us. We hid them from the cats. What to do with prayer?

Decades after the civil war, we enter the sniper's hole, sew
the sandbags, read words for his boyfriend on the wall, true with prayer.

Write my name & invite me to a wedding. I want a parade
of cars with hazards on, each blinking red, two times two with prayer.

Dear Eurydice, what good's a heart that can't resist looking back?
Foolish, music-laden Orpheus. Almost saved you with prayer.

In the museum of memory, the missing accumulate.
They carve through the tiles like grass blades, eager, damp & new with prayer.

I found a photo in a library book: lovers holding hands.
I felt chosen, then lost it. & I didn't pursue with prayer.

When I interviewed God, I said I moved the plants toward the light,
forgot the water. Is love a lack, always imbued with prayer?

Tarot cards, make me beautiful. Abundance me, O Three of Cups,
spin luck O Wheel of Fortune, I'm through, I'm through, I'm through with prayer.

# 1

# There, There, Grieving

> Where are you from?
> *There.*
> Where are you headed?
> *There.*
> What are you doing?
> *Grieving.*
>
> —Rabia al-Adawiyya

Little brother, we are all grieving
& galaxy & goodbye. Once, I climbed inside
the old clock tower of my hometown
& found a dead bird, bathed in broken light,
like a little christ.

Little christ of our hearts, I know
planets light years away
lie under our tongues. We've tasted them.
We've climbed staircases saying, *There, there.*

Little brother, we are all praying. Every morning,
I read out loud but not loud enough
to alarm anyone. Once, my love said, *Please*
*open the door. I can hear you talk. Open the door.*

Little christ of our hearts, tell anyone
you've been talking to god & see
what happens. Every day,
I open the door. I do it by looking
at my daughter on a swing—
eyes closed & crinkled, teeth bared.
I say, *Good morning good morning you*
*little beating thing.*

Little brother, we are all humming.
More & more, as I read, I sound
like my father with his book of prayers,

turning pages in his bed—a hymn
for each day of the week, a gift
from his mother, who taught me
the ten of diamonds is a win, left me
her loose prayer clothes. *Bismillah.*

Little christ of our hearts, forgive me,
for I loved eating the birds with lemon,
& the sound of their tiny bones. But I couldn't
stomach the eyes of the fried fish.

Little brother, we are always hungry.
Here, this watermelon. Here, some salt
for the tomatoes. Here, this song
for the dead birds in time boxes,
& the living. That day in the clock tower,
I saw the city too, below—

     the merchants who call, the blue awnings,
     the corn carts, the clotheslines, the heat,
     the gears that turn, & the remembering.

# ode to the afternoon

my friend tells me she's been running
in the cemetery in the afternoon
she calls it *just-a-garden-really*
first i am afraid & then i am afraid
everything is cemetery & garden
my late uncle's flower shop
my daughter learning to fold a paper into a boat
sea salt marriage dawn old french music
this vertical line digging deeper
into my forehead each morning
that bicycle in the city tied to a street post
with flowers & a note to the girl who rode it

when i was a little girl i wanted to bury the afternoon
when longing was long & my parents slept & slept
i stood in the corridor & repeated *i i i i i* until *i*
flickered in & out of myself some days *i* even

threatened to fling my body from the balcony until
my brother with such calm looked at me
dangling from the railing my head thrown backward
& explained *you don't own your soul*
*it belongs to God only He can decide*

i stood in the corridor i stood on the balcony
i stood in the desolate afternoon & repeated
because what is repetition
if not a question the way mom every day
with her hair dryer with her grocery list
with her buying this shawl & that
is asking *what have i done what have i done*

the book says we will see clearly
when the drunkenness of death descends
my uncle saw a man & a woman

standing by his hospital window
& asked his wife who they were

my father with his prayer beads
with his cigarette gestured to the driver
taking my uncle to his grave
to circle back & pass
by his flower shop my father
with his few words said
*one last time so he*
by *he* my father meant both
his brother & himself

my uncle taught me to sing *que sera sera*
he said *say it what will be will be*
i still dread the afternoon & still ask
*will i be pretty will i be missed*
& i still haven't been
to his grave but have driven
past his flower shop again & again & again
the way on the night he died i drove beneath bridges
& saw him on each one & waved

# Ghazal: Hands

Do you pine for photograph-worthy limbs, slender hands?
I asked about the soul & mom said God has tender hands.

I worried I'd need a ladder to climb up to heaven.
Or a strong grip. Or an ancestor to send her hands.

I've watched them shatter window glass. I've watched
them knead flour, water, grief. Render, hands.

Their earthly veneer tells time & the weather. Show us
how love. How green. How remorse. O calendar hands.

What medicine for longing? Salt water lifting
the breathing body. Sun, skin. Scent of lavender. Hands.

The child lets go, charges out to the sea alone. Come
dark, she drifts to her mother's touch, bends her hands.

The mother recites into the child's palm: O bird how
to eat you? Tickle. O apple tree leaves. Remember hands.

If you wave goodbye. If you wave come back. If you twirl
enough, will you learn to welcome surrender, hands?

# Pilgrim

I see you collect the scatter of houses
that abandoned you. Friend, I see
you lick the backs of photographs
like stamps & still they fall from
your shoulders. In this one you are young—
before countries & children. Sit down.
Like you, I collect what worries me. Fatherlands
are ominous & comforting like the eyes
of those who love us, & my city is a leash
that suffocates me the farther I stray
from the Mediterranean between the buildings.
The swing sings its rust in the wind.
Neither water nor stone will do. I've given up
cigarettes & libations, I separate the jars
on the bookshelves—these are for the ash
& these for the pickled cheap icons.
No matter how much vinegar I pour,
the Marys never close their eyes. No matter
how many times dawn is slaughtered,
I cry when the minarets crow.

# daily

كلّ يوم

my little country is not enough

وطني الصغير لا يكفيني

here the rain
is the peasant's god
& the driver's curse

الطرقات غرقٌ
وسائق التاكسي لا يكترث
أنَّ ضحكته أقرب إلى السعال

no remedy but
antidepressants & prayer

لا علاج هنا سوى
المهدّئات والصلاة

here even the atheist prays
for prayer is a sport
like smoking in the morning
& prayer is an art
like singing in mourning

واللغة دون الله لا توق فيها
& language without
god lacks longing

& everyone knows the only answer
to all difficult questions is

to give thanks

الحمد لله الحمد لله

my little country is not enough

وطني الصغير لا يكفيني

i abandon it every day & i return
then abandon it again
carrying, always, bags of pine nuts

أمرُّ برائحة البنزين في المحطات
أمرُّ برائحة طلاء الأظافر في الصالونات
أمرُّ برائحة الغبار في الدكان قرب البيت
أحمل حقيبة اليد السوداء

& a tin of olive oil in its wooden coffin
so the airport security would let me through
(put anything in a coffin & they'll let you through)

القمامة على الأرصفة
والصنوبر في الأكياس
وكلُّ لقاءٍ بداية
لرحيل

my little country is not enough
وطني الصغير لا يكفيني

i lose it every day on purpose & weep
i whisper *come back follow the bread scent*
*follow the lemon & minefields*
*follow the wailing of the ambulance*
*follow the songs of the dead & the living*

الأغنيات في شجر المدينة
والموت المضيء في المقاهي

i lose it every century every hour
& it returns every exile saying *remember*

هذا المشفى حيث ولدت
ما زال يحرس بكاء
الأمهات والأطفال

*these vagabond days are old are new*
*like the poet's love for balconies*

هذه الأيام قديمةٌ جديدة
كحُبّ الشاعر للشرفات

# triptych: you & my country & i

هذه كلّها بلادي...وفيها كلّ شيء...إلا أنا و بلادي

*—عبد الله البردوني

| | | |
|---|---|---|
| under the kitchen light | have you noticed | my lipstick |
| your head full of whiskey | we chant بلادي / biladi / my countries | how 70s |
| your sweat how you melt | for بلدي / baladi / my country | how predictable this hurt |
| how your chin hangs lower | is my country | neither poppy nor earth |
| neither young nor old | multitudinous or | just your daily |
| turning turning | it is infinite | this longing |
| inside this unforgiving | is it a trench | this tongue |
| consider | is بلدي only masculine no | both are possible |
| laughter & the evening | is بلادي feminine because | inside the rib cage |
| the humming | what woman doesn't know | the burning |
| of the refrigerator | the bodies the bodies | the crying |
| & all this talk | within | without |
| about what we inherit | the body the body | the bread |
| & what land now | i wonder | is just spill |
| take off your shoes | & your toes | & my nails |
| aren't they beautiful | aren't they beautiful | aren't they beautiful |

* Note: The Arabic quote above is by Yemeni poet Abdullah al-Baradouni, and it would roughly translate as "All this is my country . . . and in it / there's everything . . . except myself and my country."

# Dear white critic,

رفيقي في الرحيل،

If I told you I do not choose to write
about war & the children, would you believe me?

مللتُ القرع على أبواب الإمبراطوريات—

I'm tired of knocking on the doors of empires.

If I told you these words are
not in English, would you believe me?

لم أدرك أني كنت أقرع حتى
تكسّرت عظام أصابعي.
مللت، فعدت
وأكملت العبور

Though & because it confuses the tongue,
let me repeat this: the flowers are ours the flowers
are ours the flowers are ours.

وتأكّدت أنّ القلب عضلة
واللغة عضلة—
لِمَ كلّ هذا الاندهاش أمام مرونتنا إذاً؟
ولِمَ الركود؟

Yes the earth turns & there is time between us,
but my universe is neither corner
nor as dark as you've called it. Do you believe me?

الزيتون قليلٌ هذه السنة.
كلّما فتحتُ المرطبان
تذكّرتُ مدرستي الصغيرة وراء الشجر:

One of the boys, I
climbed over the school wall & jumped
into the olive grove.

أهديت حبيبي الأول حبّةً خضراء من هناك.
I gifted my first love a green pit.


ألا تضجرك الاستعارات عن السلام
I'm tired of metaphors about peace.


I prefer dark chocolate in the morning,
& a good window.


والشجرة المقدسة في الكتاب الأبديّ؟
ما أجمل الشتاء والباصات والحُبَّ اليافع!
جلست قرب صمتي هذا الصباح


Today I got a massage & painted
white petals on two red nails.
Do you believe me?


فلقت أرغفة الخبز وأعدتها إلى الكيس
قتلت نملةً صغيرةً في المطبخ
وكلّمتُ الله.


I don't know if I envy God his existence
outside of time, or if he envies my angst
inside the body.
لا أدري إن كنت أحسده على وجوده
خارج الزمن، أو أنه يحسدني على اضطرابي
داخل الجسد.


If I told you I'm not that other
Arab poet you've read, would you believe me?
Do I thank you for your interest?


كثيراً ما تصطفي ذاكرتي
أرجوحةً صدئةً
على شرفةٍ قديمةٍ
في الطابق السادس
أو صوت حليم
في غرفة الجلوس الحمراء

Do my names tire you? Good.
My cities are cities & my singers are singers.
Go google.

ومع أني أخاف الموت بعد كلّ أغنيةٍ

This is the first & last poem I speak to you.

لا يداهمني الوقت ولا يغريني التفسير.

Yes I believe in bridges.
If reading maps didn't bore me,
I would have learned it.

ربّما أتعلّم يوماً الرسم على الحجر
أو قيادة زورقٍ صغيرٍ، أو الوقوف على يديّ
أو تنبّؤ السعادة.

Sometimes I read the horoscopes
because I love my horns.

ربّما آخذ قيلولةً تحت شمس المدينة.

Goodbye now.
سأودّعك الآن

I banish I banish you from these lines.

قبل أن يصل أصدقائي
ونرفع نخب هذا المساء.

# Everything Here Is an Absolute

*Bar Farouk, Beirut, 2016 perhaps*

Look at where this nostalgia has brought us. We go down the stairs
& order frozen margaritas. It's been years since
we've lived here. The waiter shows us
our table, hopes we don't mind two American boys
sitting with us. There's no space for them elsewhere in this
cabaret called Metro in a capital without metros.
We say we don't mind. We are used to this city of small spaces
into which everything fits. The foreign students are our age
about a decade ago. They tell us their names & I decide to call them
Ahmad & Faysal. They agree. As the performers go onstage,
as the songs & smoke rise, we raise a toast & Ahmad & Faysal smile
& clap nonstop. They've even learned the Arab shoulder shimmy.
Once I've margarita-ed enough I start explaining
song lyrics—*She's warning him he will regret & it's no disaster
if he leaves, & yes motor is pronounced motore* & suddenly
I discover I don't really know who Zayn al-Abideen is
though I've been singing for him all my life. *Yay yay yay*
needs no interpretation. Neither do the colorful costumes
& feathers & all this going back in time. I want to shout
no one eats hummus with carrots, & no one calls this
pita bread, it's just bread, *khobz*, because everything here
is an absolute. Faysal says *thank you* & I remember
one expression for *thank you* is *May your hands
be safe & sound.* Then I ask, *Doesn't Beirut
remind you of New York?* His silence is polite,
to which I argue there are no fire escapes here,
but there could have been. Some cities burn faster than others.
I Beiruted East Houston at first sight & my friend
disagreed & said streets were making me delirious again.
What I mean is if you write your name on a wall & find it
gone, you say, *My name has left.* Would you feel abandoned?
Would you trace it again? What I mean is there are songs
where the fallen don't have rope enough to climb out of wells,
& there are songs where lovers return when the night deepens.

# Revolution Song

*For Lebanon, October 2019*

With raised fists, with floods of fury, with ululation,
with forbidden song, with the 8:00 p.m. clatter of pots and pans,
with heartbreak, with memes, with rapture, with hands, we call this revolution.

How you laugh, how you march,
how you rest, how you run, how you get caught
in your dangerous hope. No one can wall this revolution.

And love is difficult, and love is divine. And if you must
have God, let it be love. Let it be love with its toil and terror,
let it be love with its prophecy and mess,
let it be love with its rise and fall. This revolution

is now like our bodies, is eternal like dust. Is on balconies, is on screens,
is in beds, is on streets, is in the mind, is in the mind, is in the mind,
is in the breath and the eyeball, this revolution.

Praise the candle flames and the tire fumes
praise the graffiti and the broken glass
praise the names of cities and villages
praise the old man who leans on his cane and chants
praise the young man who pounds on the wall (is he crying?)
praise the detainees who won't be beaten into silence
praise those who wait for them under the rain
praise this October birth, every month be October,
every year, every ache and balm be October,
praise the dancing and the sweat and the tired feet
praise the swearing and the red flare and the rage
praise, praise it all, this revolution.

Close the roads and open them. Occupy the streets—
bring the tires, the sofas, the drums, the blaring cars.
Close the dead palaces of power and resurrect
the abandoned places, the squares, that infinite

country inside you. Close the roads and open them.
Close the classrooms and open the tents,
bring vinegar and cloth, bring your hurt and your tongue,
let it wreck and awaken and enthrall, this revolution.

The name is thawra, and thawra is woman. The woman who kicked
the thug in the gut, the woman they came for with sticks,
the woman they came for with law,
the woman who fed and the woman who prayed,
who kissed her lover on the street, who steadied her child on her waist,
who waved from the old building in her nightgown and white hair,
who scolded the soldier, who slept on the bridge,
who explained on the mic, who wailed above the blood,
call her, my people, call her

thawra

ثورة

ثورة

call this revolution.

# ode to fear of

| laughter | how gently | it prophesies wound |
| wound | how arduously | it becomes beauty |
| beauty | how effortlessly | it solicits worship |
| worship | how heartlessly | it cries god |
| god | how silently | she inhabits the body |
| the body | how desperately | she longs to b |

e        a

n            l

g      i      i  l

u

a        v

o

# 2

○

# Poem Beginning & Ending with My Birth

My mother says I sure was heaven-sent
& determined on making her life hell—
cried every afternoon, & not one spell
worked. She rocked, she sang, made all the attempts
of too-young mothers. Don't they say the scent
of a mother's neck, & her voice, soothe well?
The familiar heartbeat's supposed to tell
the story of the womb. Not how it went.
Until one day she put me in a chair
with a newspaper to tear out & toss
into a water bucket. Algebra
or God happened (quiet, I tore), & where
does it end? She recognized it, this loss,
she swears, the morning I was born. She saw.

She swears the morning I was born she saw
the dishes stacked, though the news wasn't dry.
The war brought the dead, the mothers the cries
of newborns. The militias made the laws:
cross here, here stop, here knock, here dance, here draw
a card—spades or hearts? Your fate does not lie
in your hands or the Almighty's. The eye
of the gun is multi-pupiled. *Blah blah*
went the angels, though they watched over us,
didn't they? Or did *we* come to our aid?
Some smoked. *Where's the crossword?* asked the grandpas.
Everyone smoked, blamed each other, the bus,
& every pregnant woman was afraid
she'd soon be in labor, all back & jaws.

I'd soon be in labor, all back & jaws,
though less after the epidural. God
bless the anesthesiologist! No rod
of *in pain you will*, your unholy laws.
Stab my spine painless or I'll dig my claws

into your jugular. Don't you applaud
the sacrifice of mothers, don't you God
them. Altars are for the dead, & rage gnaws
at us: we're badass, & what we want? We
know. & we don't know. None of your business.
Both times I prayed for a girl, & intent
birthed them, as it did my mother & me;
we're our own expulsion—& genesis,
moments later. We begin our dissent.

Moments later, we began our descent
down the building stairs. There was no shelter;
we hid in the school next door. We entered,
played with the older kids, who sometimes lent
us their Risk game set. Confused, we still went
with it. We loved the colors, & better,
the dice. We rolled. Hunched into our laughter,
we counted losses. My mother's lament
came not from missiles, but from sudden news
of her brother's death. He, countries away,
engineer, hit his head on the cement.
She'd seen him in a dream. How does God choose
when to show us, when to keep us at bay?
She saw her brother's face, saw herself bent.

She saw her brother's face. We saw her bent
over his photo, or a soapy plate.
Heard her light her last cigarette so late
it was early. Morning, between the rent
& electricity, to what extent
does one have time to mourn? Who derails fate,
peace? The only train I'd seen didn't wait—
abandoned in the city grass, content
in the apocalypse. I spent most days
on the balcony: next door, the immense
emptiness of the archbishopric called.
I imagined running in the always
of its sun-flood until mother's voice pressed.
I tied my blue laces, postponed my awe.

I tied my blue laces, & to my awe,
it never worked. I loved September best:
without fail, rain the clear illusionist
fell on the first day of school, always brought
the earth with it: the soil's fragrance rose raw
even in the alley. We chewed fast, lest
our mom find out what we'd bought with the rest
of our money. Remember? The hurrah
as we quickly ate the cake-filled brioche?
& the rotary phone? & my love for
new stationery, my fear of chamois
shoes? Tights torn, soaked, too wholehearted, too gauche,
too rushed. I tried to hide it all before
we walked in, but tying my shoes, she saw.

I walked in & she tied my shoes. She saw
the dirt, & sometimes shouted. But she let
me find & lose my Edens, alphabet
after alphabet. When boredom would gnaw,
she said, *Read the dictionary.* No flaw
in scarcity, if the mind wills. Duet
of languages, thank you. Thank you, cassette,
& TV ads—I memorized them all.
Today she called, said her mother isn't
dying. Perhaps she should? Didn't she wolf
most her days? Enough. She can't invent
excuses for her again. She wasn't
kind. She dreaded the visit, thinking of
how the whole day would go. & still she went.

How the whole day would go, & how it went
depended on the inflatable boat,
the cold river, the warm mountain, its coat
of marguerites, & our careful descent
into the summer morning. We'd no tent,
too young to camp, happy to be remote
from parents & the city. An old goat
grazed, & strangely it lightened my torment,

my fear of the wild. Then you turned—did you?
In a lost diary, a girl writes this;
*We walked off, briefly, but alone at least.*
*The others set the picnic, called. I knew.*
I can't know it as well as she, that kiss.
She tells it like an oracle, a priest.

She tells this like an oracle, a priest:
*I see you. You'll be a writer, one day.*
*I see you. You will stand up, read, & they*
*will listen to your words. & from the east*
*to the west to the south you'll go, released*
*of directions. When God loves you, your way*
*will be cleared. He'll show you his land. I'll pray*
*for you always.* A mother's words, like yeast,
make the dreams rise. She said this as I ate,
then turned to her pot. The kitchen was so
full of sun that grains of dust danced supreme.
Is this how we dive straight into our fate?
What we must summon when we're filled with no,
when we doubt, when we say, *Perhaps a dream?*

When we doubt, when we say, *Perhaps a dream,*
our grandma doesn't blink. We know her eye
is plastic—the spare one in a box, high
on top of the closet. & in the gleam
of the afternoon, inside the thick cream
of her voice, we listen: Jesus walked by
her bed & said nothing. She wonders why,
though they who behold his face are redeemed.
& so we spent nights praying for someone
biblical to arrive, like a rock star.
We hummed, waited. No one came to visit.
Our grandmother told stories & was gone.
She returns when we doubt the past, the far,
when we laugh, joke, & make nothing of it.

When we laugh, joke, & make nothing of it,
the unseen laughs more. Here's mom with photos
we take & no longer print. When she shows
my brothers & me, opens the closet,
takes the albums out, her eyes, they soften,
they long to wake something in us that knows.
*Look how you cry, how you smile, how you close*
*yourself when you're mad. Remember? Often*
*we fought & you slammed your bedroom door. You*
*hid. We couldn't find you. Strange how I see*
*you inside your little daughter.* If peace
came, it didn't linger. & is it true,
what she recalls, what I recall, what we?
She insists it's real. The truth. Every piece.

She insists it's real, the truth, every piece,
though I don't remember myself this tense.
My daughter, my lovely wreck, my immense,
forgive me this day my daily. Release
me not from anger, from error, but please
know trains run in me, & many dead. Sense
sometimes deserts me. Fogged, fickle, my lens.
Hallowed be thy name. Cedar-like, thy trees.
Thy kingdom come. Thy kingdom come, though don't
forget palms who raised you to the window
so you could see the rain. Who heard your scream
first. I sound desperate because I am. Won't
lie. Won't stop. O dear magnificent glow,
don't you see your mother, lonely, supreme?

Don't you see us mothers, lonely, supreme?
—Prophecies never prevented murder.
What use to scribble over a border?
—Mistook rioting for writing. Extreme
much? What do you fear most, in the grand scheme
of things? —Tyranny of stories. Ardor.
Mistook backwash for: laundry, leftover.
Eden for a dictatorial regime.

Tonight the cities to be bombed will be
bombed. The mothers will die little deaths. More
than anything, they'll long for their coffins
on shoulders. Is worship mutual, free?
Doesn't matter, does it? Who's keeping score?
We're birthing (what difference?) sinners, prophets.

We're birthing (what difference?) sinners, prophets,
daughters of war & dance cities. Heaven
opens its gates at birth, she says. Seven
skies. What are we without longing. Comets,
aluminum foil in our hair. Solace
comes & goes. I wake. Was it to lessen
my angst she came in a dream? I reckoned
there'd be crying. There was. In the province
of love & anger, in kitchens, in fields
of fitted sheets, she told & she shouted,
mainly to Mary. O mother, she meant
what she said. & though she knows nothing shields,
though in her mad devotion she doubted,
my mother says I sure was heaven-sent.

My mother says I sure was heaven-sent.
She swears the morning I was born she saw
she'd soon be in labor, all back & jaws.
Moments later, I began my dissent.
She saw my brother's face, saw herself bent,
tying his blue laces, & to her awe,
my brother walked in. She tied his shoe. Saw
how the whole day would go, & so it went.
She tells this like an oracle, a priest.
When we doubt, when we say, *Perhaps a dream*,
when we laugh, joke, & make nothing of it,
she insists it's real. The truth. Every piece.
Don't you see us mothers, lonely, supreme?
We're birthing (what difference?) sinners, prophets.

# Bulbul

Forgive me. I've come back to you
without letters. When I recite I get stuck on خ.
When I fill out my daughters' school forms
about languages spoken at home, I lie:

    1.   Arabic
    2.   English
    3.   French

I forget the order of your alphabet though I know
all the old Egyptian plays by heart. By heart by pencil
I attempt to return.

    خ like خالي / empty
    like خيار / choice
    like خبز / bread
    like خردة / junk

I dream in Lebanese. I count in French.

    Un. You
    Deux. English
    Trois. French


Do you love the rain?
The students turned their umbrellas
to a Sinatra song in Beirut & here I am
writing to you about pining for New York City. Unashamed
tourist, pulled from Penn Station to the Empire State
& once at the top I cried, no, bawled
& Huda filmed me & laughed. I digress.
The Iraqi auntie at the book fair insisted I read
in Arabic. Instinctively my hands went for my pockets
like someone fumbling for change or a magician about to pull out
a long colorful handkerchief & a dove. An apology
fluttered out of my mouth & the auntie shook her head.
Where is my shovel? Where is the cemetery?
The bones I rummage for are buried in
my muscles, & most of my molars are gone. Bad teeth.

When the bulbul on our balcony flew away, my father
reassured me it would come back. I waited; the cage
remained خالي , so I tattooed the bird on my back.
With two mirrors, I am able see it, but most days I strain
my neck & eyeballs, twist my right shoulder, look back.

The necklace I chose at the shop was difficult to fasten.
My friend said trust there will always be loving hands
behind you, so I made my خيار : which direction?

When your refrains ripen I eat them like خبز ,
though I keep boarding airplanes to cold places.
The yearning & the migrating know guilt
guilt guilt guilt guilt accumulates like خردة.

I'll build from it a temple & go worship somewhere else.

# أزرق blue

نرى البحر ولا نراه
إلّا في المنام

a patch a glimpse
among the antennas

أو من بين الأشرطة على الأسطح

how to brave this blue?

لا بحر لنا هنا ولا قوّة

sometimes i forget the sea
is this close

لنا حبٌّ قديمٌ
يريد أن يحفِر لك
في الإسمنت شاطئاً
my love i want to dig
a beach for you
out of this cement

لنا مطرٌ محمّلٌ
تارةً بعطش الأرض
وتارةً بعفن الشارع

o old faith & new
o time of wells & time
of satellite dishes

لنا الحرّ والرقص على ظهور المباني
(قد نرى بقعة بحرٍ من هناك)

are the fish still edible?
our nets are full
of plastic & trash

لنا كأسٌ تجري فينا
كنبعٍ صغيرٍ
ننسُج فيه سماءً وغروباً ونجوماً وتراتيلا

my parents threw me in the sea
when I was two & I floated
they called me little fish
my parents trusted the sea

إلهنا الأزرق
لم نعد نعبده
وما زلنا نحبّه
o blue god
we no longer worship
but still love

لِمَ لا نتذكّر البحر إلّا
عندما تموت العصافير
على الشرفات؟

over breakfast i had to convince a friend
beirut was still on the mediterranean

لمن ندوّن أحلامنا كلّ صباح؟

are you sure? he asked
is it a deep bluest blue?

ما أجمل الموت بلا ضرائح!

yes, i said
no, i said

إرفعني على كتفيك
قبل أن نحرق المدينة
lift me on your shoulders
roll in the tires
light them up

o city we no longer love but still worship

لقد أقسمنا أن نُقلع عن عبادة هذه المدينة

# What the Returning Do

Three years of absence bring dead things & new love.
Here's the old house. What you smell is true, love:

bird carcass trapped between wall & flowerpot,
so you do what the returning do—love

what you pound with broomstick until
dried bones & feathers fall. Who, love,

can say if this century is worse than others?
& despite what you know & knew, love

comes back as your city, or your old friend
dipping fries in labneh. They ask you *Love*

*have you been cured or are you still*
*an optimist? Does the woman who grew love*

*& flowers inside empty gas grenades*
*still bring you hope?* They say few love

the way you do, but they forget
(it's been a while) they, too, love

olives, though they're tired of odes
& elegies. You wake & pursue love,

look in the mirror, read the news. Sometimes
you wonder how two loves

so conflicting persist. Then you remember
driving away can get you through love

& borders & some of the days. You can't predict
what time decides. How's the view, love?

# Heirloom

I come from a line of women who describe
flinging themselves into death
but don't. My grandmother always announced
what she had swallowed. Always demanded to be taken
to the hospital. Always asked for more doctors.
Which means my mother hasn't learned nothing gets fixed
by being broken over & over again. She keeps
to the sea, baptizes herself in it all year, avoids
altitudes. Once, driving around a mountain curve
at sunset, she asked, *Don't you wish you could just
drive straight into the belly of this valley?*
I rent apartments on high floors though I've seen
my body plunge. I stood on the other side
of the railing twice. This scares me. I used to disappear
into the closet for afternoons. My grandmother's
been aging beneath her blanket for decades.
My mother hid in the bathroom & thought I didn't notice.
Once, in a fit of rage, she stirred a divine scent
on the stove & carried it to her sick mother, came back
with an antique vase from her parents' house
& placed it in the glass cabinet. Engraved, throne-like.
One day I will carry that. I used to knock over
the bottles & boxes on the dresser with the back of my hand.
This scares me too. Now I walk down the street & pray
for the music. When I told my husband,
*If you listen close enough everything's dancing, try
to guess the songs*, he laughed. But I'm telling you,
beauty always comes, you hear me?
It always comes.

# Every Soul Needs Windows

The matriarch is gone. Is it accurate to say
we weren't close, if there is blood between us?
My mother sends me a photograph of time
within time within time. In the mirror
inside the photograph: her mother dying in a rented bed.
Under the mirror: a framed picture of my grandmother
dying more slowly in her rented youth.

O grandmother the gorgeous:
the elbow on the table, the bracelet on the wrist,
the smooth cheek on the fist, the kohl
in the eyes, the eyes
looking away. O grandmother the hollow:
the body in the sheets, the skin on the bones,
the thin hair on the scalp, the eyes in the sockets, still
looking away. Which disappearance is more merciful?
O grandmother the lonely, how far
are you, how far am I, from your Damascus
childhood? Behind the camera: my mother,
whom we do not see. Looking at my invisible
mother looking at her mother looking at death:
myself, of another millennium and other countries.
A desert between us. A river between us. An elegy
is an elegy is an ode. No peace between us.

The cold matriarch is gone. We've inherited
her jawline. The day before she died, she recognized
her previous self in the photograph.
"I was beautiful," she told her daughter.
We learn our lines and repeat them.
The chairs in her salon are empty because
belongings outlive us. Last week, my mother developed
pictures of my daughters. She scolds me
because I don't preserve faces behind glassine
or glass. Every soul need windows.

I'm lazy, I say, and I don't say
I'm afraid. My daughter tells me
my grandmother will return in another body,
though she won't remember. One lifetime
is never enough. Did I say cruel? Mostly to herself.
Did I mention her name? The wounding kind
of love that makes you mad, makes you thirst.

# Ghazal: My Daughter

*For Aya*

*after Marilyn Hacker*

The neonatal doctor describes you; *Champion, no doubt,* my daughter.
Two days old, hands tied—tried to pull your breathing tube out, my daughter.

What rush you were in to leave the womb! No one told me the real odds were
not with us. You in the incubator, & I without my daughter.

Your grandmother canceled the chocolates. No, *postponed* was her word, for she
believed in angels, & I sang you ABBA like a devout, my daughter.

When the gyno cut, I was full of god & nausea. Quickly they pulled
you out of me & the room. Said my uterus was drought, my daughter.

The first few hours your alveoli expanded, did not collapse.
I fell asleep, woke up breathless, knew what that was about, my daughter.

Two doses of surfactant & a central IV. O but your eyes:
how you breathed with them, my tiny, my defiant, my stout, my daughter.

What could I, slashed & IV-ed, shaky under the blankets, breasts useless,
do but wait, then leave, then water my visits with song. Sprout, my daughter.

The scent of hand sanitizer. The drive to the hospital. Today
they removed your ventilator. *Surprise!* the nurse shouts. My daughter,

we named you Aya, a line from the Qur'an, the Bible. *Your beauty's*
*light, an aya,* goes the song. I believe: I hear your صَوت, my daughter.

# Flamingos

*For Leina*

As the nurses pushed your bed into the OR,
you extended your arms toward us, & we promised
we'd take you to see the flamingos
in the hospital garden downstairs.
When you woke up, you refused to pee
on the diaper underneath you (you'd been potty-trained
for months), so we brought the bedpan & explained
you couldn't walk yet, but soon. I learned
to listen to your monitor in my sleep.
The worried aren't supposed to be hungry,
but I ordered food because it was reassuring
to know there was someone grilling chicken
in a restaurant in the city in the outside,
which still existed. I decided to google Lady Gaga
& watch her videos. I contemplated dyeing
my hair red. The day they took you out of the ICU, I left

to take a shower at home. On my way
to the kitchen, my hair dripping, my arms full
of laundry, for a second I must have forgotten
my step, twisted & cracked my ankle.
I hollered until the pain settled. Your father
was with you. Your grandmother held
your little sister & called out to God. I called
a friend & leaned on him until we reached the car.
In the ER, all I could do was laugh. I who can barely handle
a blood test, or a mild fever, or even
ultrasound gel on my stomach,
I who can't hold still enough
for an X-ray, laughed & told the doctor
to fix my ankle, quick, I have a daughter
waiting in a room upstairs, yes, here, in *this* hospital,

isn't this funny? This is not about heroism.
This is not about selflessness, for you know too well
how many times I've refused to play cards with you,
how many times I've failed to listen, how I obsess
& disappear in search of words I don't always
understand. Perhaps this is an apology. Perhaps I'm saying
life will sometimes infect your daughter's lung
& fracture your ankle in the same week.
& most days, the car doesn't break down,
& the children are healthy, & your husband
loves you, but you will be terrified nevertheless,
& sometimes empty. It's ok if you forget
to put one foot in front of the other. & please
call me. I love you. I will tell you again
about that afternoon we both sat in wheelchairs,
I with my leg cast, you with your IV,
ate mashed potatoes, watched the flamingo
sculptures, which you probably knew couldn't
be entirely delivered from the stone they're made of,
but still pointed, *Look, mama*—
this one is bending toward the water,
this one is balancing on one leg,
this one is about to fly.

# Time,

be kind to her. She's eleven & already
wants to turn you back. She wished this
after she squeezed a drop from her index
& read me the number. She always insists
I close my eyes & guess
what her blood is saying—
sometimes I'm wrong & sometimes not.

I kiss the tiny tears on her fingertips.
I kiss her arms & thighs before the insulin.
When I ask her to inject herself, I'm asking her to live
without me, & she knows it. When her legs trembled,
& I soothed with "I'm here, I'm here,"
she reminded me: "But you can't do anything."
Perhaps she meant "undo."

Who am I kidding. Time, I demanded your undoing too,
that first night in the hospital before dawn,
when I woke up having forgotten, then remembered
where I was, what had happened—
the neon corridor light, the nurses' chatter,
the potassium's slow burn in my daughter's vein.

Time, I know
I can't reason with you. You go on & on.
Instead, I'm wishing her
astonishing slowness, softness
inside the arduous & unfair. Like this:

the dog's limp, the cold coffee, the struggling
baby bougainvillea, the winged ant on the floor,
the half-eaten sandwich, the tenderness
of the 5:00 a.m. light, the daily departures,
the basil plant's shadow on the wall,
& her hair, the swing of my love's hair

as she runs, shaking her head
left & right, left & right,
how she always ran like this, always ran
as if swaying, No, No.

(For Aya, September 2021)

# 3
○

# Conversation with Sun God

I, too, miss the cold & the murmurs of pedestrians.
Fellow rain-deprived, light-quenched, sand-hearted,
let me tell you about the afternoon my love & I
drove the car slowly to the cedars, randomed
on a warm restaurant with red pasta & wine. I don't greed
for the beauty of snow-covered mountains. Sun God,
only a little rain would douse. Your worshippers are in love
with the body & I prefer to escape it. Ethereal-seeming, they.
I don't own rain boots anymore. Don't anger
if I say I want to leave. I merely want to be
in my red trench coat on that day
we bought cheap purple plates from the $1 store.
We never used them but I still hear
their clatter in the plastic bags as we walked
under our umbrellas back to my studio,
clicked on the small heater & lay on the rug.
I miss choosing umbrella colors on sidewalks.
Were we as happy as we seemed, or do we always distort
impatient youth? Sun God, Sun God, ok
perhaps what I miss the most is the now.
My daughters just climbed into the bus,
my love is still asleep upstairs,
& I'm standing in a sweater under the heat.

# prophecy

نبوّة

do you still smoke?

نسيت كلَّ شيء لكني لم أرمِ علبة الجيتان

we never got to watch Aznavour live

مع أنّي أقلعت منذ عامين

my daughter thinks all the singers i listen to are dead
اِبنتي تعتقد أنَّ كلَّ المغنين الذين أستمع إليهم ماتوا

& i keep saying things like

هل سنعبر هذا الشارع
بعد الستين، يداً بيد، في صباح يوم أحدٍ لا شمس فيه؟
we will cross this street in our sixties, hand in hand, on a sunny sunday morning

فالمدينة لا تتذكّر أحداً

or: the city will not betray us / the city remembers what will come

والوحدة أقدم من الله

& the green parrots are migrating again

وأنا توقّفتُ عن البحث عنك
& I have not stopped looking for you

# Ghazal-Ode for My Body

Body, body, o dear ordinary miracle,

    I want. To learn how to be bold in my body.
    It's always young, it's always old in my body

& at what age does one begin? I begin.
Are you lost? Are you tide? I want you to be
September, with its promise of rain. With its prophecy
of storm. With its school buses.

    I couldn't wait to drive a car, to be alone
    inside the music & the road in my body.

Some of us stood, some of us sat. We all sang
to the driver to go fast, fast, to not be scared
of death or the police, for we are the children
of this city. Body, body, are you city or bus?

    My voice fills a room, a stage. But the louder is
    the more reticent, the untold in my body.

I am afraid of mirrors, & my profile,
the rise & fall of it. My husband knows
I hate my shape in pajamas;
he orders oversize men's shirts,
leaves them on the bed, texts,
*Size came out wrong, you can sleep in this one.*
I know he desires me, & that I am beautiful. & yet
I am the man inside me who longs for the skinny woman.

    Body, elegiac & comic dog. I pet
    & pity, delighted & bored in my body.

On days I love me, I take photos of myself.
On days I don't, I zoom in & out, envy the me

of last week. How do I pine for what almost still is?
How do I mourn what's not dead? Body, body, I want
to know what we look like to others. Sometimes I point
to a woman on the street & ask my husband, my friends,
*Is this me? Is this me?*

>    The clothesline shirts shift. The church bells say *Sunday, sun,*
>    *this day, light* crosses the threshold in my body.

My aunt takes out her teeth to eat the fish.
She loves my shoulders, those headstones
under which so much is buried
above which two angels sit
& write, like me. Angels, angels, tell me
what good, what bad have I done today? Tell me

>    *Will it hurt?* An ancient question. Still, I'm afraid
>    of bees, words, the sea, & the cold in my body.

Before she learned to speak, my daughter
caught a bee in the grass & cried.
The neighbors brought a garlic clove. My daughter forgot.
We used to hum to a bee, *Your house has fallen on your children,*
to scare her into leaving. Do I teach this song to my daughters?

>    I told the rain, *If I must leave, stop now.* It stopped,
>    I stayed. A miracle (behold!) in my body.

The curtains in my hospital room are full of red roses.
In the elevator, the old man in the wheelchair holds
in his lap a decaying red folder. We nod at each other.
I tell my husband, *If you ever buy me red roses, I'll kill you.*

>    For months, no hunger. I pray for it, though did I
>    not want to weigh less, be adored in my body?

Body, body, if you're form, if you're space,
if you're color, matter, light, tool, time,

are you not art? & must I not love you?
When the electricity cuts, must I not
keep reciting my lines in the dark?

The pigeon bumped into my window all morning—
escape? Perseverance? What code in my body?

Hello dust, childhood companion. Hello, god
of un-clocks. When I was a little girl, watching dust
was my favorite prayer. Back then, I seemed bodiless.
Body, body, when did the loathing start?

I haven't been good to me. I eat, stretch, begin
the slow labor. Where is the Lord? In my body.

When I thought of you as border, I asked
my slender mother, *Would you swap bodies, if we could?*
She said yes & was afraid every time I stood on the balcony.
When we were younger, she was afraid for our corneas,
my brother & I, playing archery with rope & wire hangers.
*Be careful*, she said. *Be careful for your eyes*,
though she should have warned us about our shoulders.
On the way to the hospital today, my husband & I
saw a turtle cross the narrow road.
We slowed down, considered it a good omen.

In the future of the future, will I be named
Z, recite the broken ode in my body?

My daughter says *remember* instead of *remind*,
as in, *Remember me of that song?*
I lather my limbs with scented oil, smell
the church that I am. What was I
saying? Remember me of, remember me.

# Say it,

a man your grandfather's age ____ you,
& years later you couldn't kiss your boyfriend
without ____, no matter how tender his eyes.
You've tried, you've tried not to ___, but fuck it,
say fingers say callous laughter say lap. You were nine & these
were non-breasts. & when you told your mom she ___,
& she said not to tell your dad because your dad would
___ him, & you believed her. & when your mom told his wife
the wife said it was just ____, & she did not believe that.
& so it was & you all lived & thank G_d at least no one said
it was your fault, at least you were never left
alone with him again (except in the real of your mind,
reel enough to flicker for decades), at least he didn't ___ you.
What happened? You know you can do this, you are ___,
the ___ will come if you just ___. You kept putting on
rage & weight. Perhaps you wanted to be ___. Your father,
who has a piece of bread & a spoon of honey for breakfast,
shook his head & told you the Prophet says ____, says we are a people who

*don't eat to be full. We eat so we do not go hungry. Less, my daughter, less.*

___ give me, father, for I am ravenous & ___,
I ___ this world so much I want to ____ it.
I peeled the new polish off my fingernails, & the old green paint
off the shutters. I have an inexplicable ___ for shutters
& all things all things, except my hips. Once, I took apart
the tiara you bought me, bright stone by bright—
it was so beautiful & I cried. I long to eat
the smell of onion when it sizzles sweet
in the olive oil. Sometimes I ask myself whether I
____ him now that he's dead, but fuck that.
(In the book of days, *does* comes before *dies*.)
Even the fearsome black lion in my dream
was delicious silk. Look
how fierce I've become.

# triptych: voice

| | | |
|---|---|---|
| at 36 my body | & i speaking again | like a teenage boy |
| my voice deepening | a coarser tone | possessed |
| here in the throat | i the big-boned girl | always was |
| i remember all | long hair inside cap | when i played basketball |
| that day | my boyfriend told me | mom didn't recognize me then did |
| *my girl here* | *your beautiful shoulders* | she stroked my hair |
| | | |
| my neighbor touched | my knees thighs | i couldn't name what |
| my chest shut | windowless i | toughened my walk |
| shoulders first | feet shuffling | always in a V |
| became half-bison | half-flightless | bird no one wants |
| he felt & felt | he praised & praised | i told mom |
| then stopped when | i noticed the | green beans in her lap |
| i smiled twisted removed | tight strings | quickly so we forget |
| his hands | in our throats | don't wreck the afternoon |
| | | |
| my now-voice & i | we unfold say map | took long for me to |
| watch palms & spine | drop & break dance | balance crown on the floor |
| turn release | lifting yes we lift | pray the body diagonal |
| the body open | the body holy | the god-body |
| yet i'm still afraid | when i touch | my Adam's apple |
| i practice | my music box | one vowel at a time |
| what is a girl | what is this sound | what is this voice |
| if not skin | if not air | if not dance |
| if not light | rushing | rush |
| | | |
| rushing | from the lungs | from the lungs |

# Souk

The soldiers are afraid
of the camera. *Are you shooting the souk?*
The photographer says *No no, just her.*
I say *Just me, just me.*
My black dress, a little above the knee, helps.
A girl learns to spectacle enough.
The soldier nods, lowers his head.
The crew remind me to say

*Not from here,* to say *Half-half,*
to speak English, mostly.
*Everyone is always kinder to strangers.*
The city devours her children,
unless she doesn't recognize them.

And so I, of this city,
I who stand on stages and name this city,
deny this city in the heart of the city,
deny this city at the old gate of the city.
I say *Bonjour* I say *Thank you* I undo
my accent. When you say hometown, what do you mean?

The crew comment on the quality
of the light through the tin roofs,
they say *Pretend no one is looking.*
But the guy with the espresso and cigarette is looking,
and the teenager who sells batteries is looking,
and the man with the shisha is looking, and the woman
in the clothes shop, his wife perhaps, is looking.
The photographer says *Beautiful* says *Try*
*to keep your shoulders even.* I cross and uncross
my arms, remind him it's time for my second outfit.
A girl learns not to spectacle too much.

The store owner who's given us space to change
tells me the story of this ancient street,
tells me about the shootings a few years ago,
says *And they were all neighbors,*
says *Nothing works, nothing works,*
says his uncle comes here every morning
just to bathe and feed this kitten.
I do not tell him I heard the fire from my house.
I raise my eyebrows. I shake my head.
I code switch I dress switch
I silent I carnival I hypocrite.
When you say blasphemy, what do you mean?

The looks are lighter when I'm in jeans.
I stand in the center of the street,
remember to give way to the motorcycles,
give way to the old man with a bag of minced meat,
give way to the mother and two daughters.
The crew remind me to breathe
on the count of three, for a better photo.
As we pack up, someone yells, *Kiss it!*
We laugh. When you say body, what do you mean?

This is called The Wheat Market.
There used to be harvest here, once.
Sometimes names stop belonging to their children,
and does it matter? I used to think
the cemeteries were far from the city.
I used to think my shadow didn't belong to me—
my mother found me, two years old, terrified,
trying to run from it in the corridor.
I look up—1 2 3, 1 2 3,
there are stone arches,
there are posters of politicians,
there's a red lace dress
flagging on the ropes above us.

# Incredible

*Incredible*, my daughter describes love, pauses after the *in*—I believe her.
If your daughter asks, *Can God be in my earrings & in the sky?*, believe her.

When your mother says, *It's cold outside, wear an undershirt & take a jacket*,
when she despairs & warns you, *You'll bite your fingers off when I die*, believe her.

A girl speaks about what she tries to forget. She says, *Him, years ago*.
& they ask: *Are you sure?* &: *Perhaps* &: *Why now?* &: *Why believe her?*

In the old map, the land is small. In the new map, the land is smaller.
When she becomes invisible, what will her children do? Try? Be? Leave her?

Your friend texts she's afraid the plane might fall.
Between laughter & goodbye, believe her.

When Father Ibrahim walks the old city, people greet him, call him *Hajj*.
Mecca is where you're willing to find her. Wherever she may lie, believe her.

Your name means *what beautifies*. Words are incredible, & love is incredible,
& seasons are incredible, & when your death arrives in July, believe her.

# Ode to Lipstick

Today, you bought new lipstick. You ate
dark chocolate, listened to a friend
rage about marriage. You saw a newborn
in a stroller & weren't moved. You're relieved
your children's legs don't wrap around your hips
anymore, they click their seat belts into place
by themselves. Your older daughter
just turned 10 & is learning
to send you messages like
"Keep Calm & Love Mama."
She imitated your dance moves in the car.
This made you feel a little immortal.

The lipstick you bought is called Plum.
It smells good. You're learning to love bolder
colors on your lips: red, mauve, fuchsia. You want
to go out one day & buy green lipstick.
There should be lipstick called "To Go Out One Day
& Buy Green Lipstick" or "I Rant About Marriage
With My Girlfriends & Laugh" or
"I Will Party Tonight" or
"Because Life Is Too Short." Except today life felt long

enough for you to go through your old makeup.
You gave your daughter the lipsticks she'd broken
& told her not to touch the new ones. You threatened,
she nodded & smiled at her gift. Life was long enough
for you to go out before sunset because you needed
tomatoes & the hypnotic light at that time of the day.
You only remembered the tomatoes when you opened the fridge
& only remembered the beautiful light when
you drove through it. The world took slower breaths
& you loved it, the way you love your children with an ache
when they're sleeping, when the quiet
makes you long for the voices

you'd silenced in the afternoon.
Or the way you whisper to your husband
in his sleep that you miss him, ask him
to remember the words in the morning,
& he doesn't. You talk about marriage.
"Only a piece of paper," he says,
& what he means is, "Don't be afraid.
Us is still here inside all this."
Who remembers anything in the morning daze?

Today you woke up anticipating the hours,
smiling in bed like a child excited about
a trip to the beach. Surprised, you asked,
"What is it, again, that I'm happy about?"
Slowly, you conjured the house
the real estate agent showed you:
empty, spacious, full of sun & dust.
Perhaps you were moved when you saw
the child. Perhaps you're saying you don't regret
not having the one that had started inside you
in December. You took the pills. You bled. You cried.
You want an empty uterus, & to dance.
You want arms strong enough to lift
this weight & the new house.
When asked to put "from" in a sentence,
your daughter wrote, "I am from my mother."
You've decided you are country enough.
The night begins. An airplane blinks in the distance.
The old & new loves wait at airports, in homes, on street curbs.
You will wear your new lipstick. Call it
"Look at Us, All Want & Tongue."
Your husband will not stand still
for a photo. You will rise when
a favorite song comes.

# Sometimes All You Can Do Is Wait

The dermatologist injects the local anesthetic
into my upper arm. When she begins to carve,

I tell her it is not enough, so she reinserts the needle for more
numbness, though she doesn't seem convinced

I'm still feeling some pain. The hope is the biopsy will help her
determine the disease, though that's not what I'd call

something so external. She promises she won't stitch,
just allow the wound to heal from the inside out.

If this is an allergic reaction, she explains,
the antihistamine should have worked,

& when I fear something parasitical from the boxes
the movers used this month, she says the rest of the family

would also be itching. *Is anyone else itching?* she repeats.
She looks unsure, but not worried.

I read about the causes of itchiness, all improbable for me:
eczema, psoriasis, scabies, lice, chicken pox, hives.

I take photos of the skin on my thigh, the side of my breast,
my arm, my calf, my belly, & send them to friends. *See?*

They reassure & recommend doctors. My mother suggests
baking soda mixed with oil or water, rosewater perhaps, perhaps

taking a cool bath. My mother-in-law says sometimes
it just goes away if you try not to scratch at all.

In my research I find out itchy skin is called *pruritus*
from Latin, seemingly related to *prurient*:

"having a restless desire or longing," or
"causing lasciviousness or lust," or "having

lustful thoughts." All neither curable
nor contagious. *Is anyone else itching?*

& this time I confess my husband worries too
about where we will retire, us runaways from

hometowns & home gods. & my children,
who call their grandparents' country *vacation,*

ask why we don't own the new house, nod
when we remind them to turn off the lights to reduce

the electricity bill, or that class friends might leave
to go back somewhere. The doctor admits she finds it difficult

to save up too, & might return to Brazil soon. *Where
do you return?* she asks. & I say too often & not enough,

& we agree to wait for the lab results on Monday.
All summer my daughter ran to my father,

who applied calamine or sprayed Spirto on her mosquito bites.
*The more you scratch them, the bigger they grow,* he told her,

& I remembered how he used to whisper to me, *Your salty blood.
That's how the mosquitoes find you, even on the sixth floor.*

# Ode to Leaving

غُربة

Sorry I've been absent.
My sister left my brother leaves
tomorrow. How r u?

مررتُ بها الساعةَ التاسعة
لنلتقي زياد ويارا في بارومتر.
ذكّرتها بالمظلّة لأنّ اللّيلَ كان يبدو ممطراً.

Beirut without you wasn't
beautiful this summer.

في طريقنا إلى البارِ الممتلئ بأغاني الثمانينات والنوستالجيا
تساءلتُ إن كنتُ قد أقلعُ عن التدخين،
أو قد أنتظر

At the airport,
& airports scar me.
What r we afraid of?

ولادة ابنةٍ لي يوماً ما.
كانت بيروتُ جميلةً كالعادة، غير آبهةٍ
بالموتِ أو الغبارِ أو بنا،

That we will age & laugh
& lose people hopefully
not too young & without much
suffering or disease?

وبالرّغم من ذلك غنّينا أزنافور.

Aznavour died today
& je n'ai pas su, je ne sais pas,

لطالما شعرتُ بأنّي أُشبهه:
أفتحُ كفّيَّ وأقبضهما في العتمةِ المضيئة

I always felt I resembled him:
opening & clenching my fists
in the light-flooded dark.

لم أعرف لم أعرف

I wonder, when the times come,
if I'd feel full. Or ready. Is anyone ever?

لن أعرفَ أبداً كيف أُسكِتُ قلباً يموت.
ضحكنا كثيراً وبكيتُ تحت قناطرِ الجامعة.
غنّينا كلّ الأشياء باستثناءِ النشيد الوطنيّ.
ربما كنّا ننتظرُ قيامةً ما.

I wonder what cities would b broken
by then & what would b rebuilt.

لم نكن نعلم آنذاك أنّنا سنهربُ
من غربةٍ إلى غربة.

U can buy Carthage or Jerusalem in small shops
& that's not even murderous.

لم أكن أعلم أنّها ستلتقطُ لي صورةً
وأنا أقفُ وراء زجاج المطارِ
المسكونِ ببصماتِ المودّعين،
ملوّحةً بيدي.
Do you still have that photo you took
of me standing behind the fingerprint-stained
airport glass, waving?

هكذا إذاً هاجرت هي إلى العالمِ الأوّل
وسافرتُ أنا إلى بلادِ البترول.
لا شيء حقيقيٌّ هنا أو هناك.

A giant tree weeps on the curbside
by my daughter's nursery.
I smoke underneath it every day, even

in the heat. Do I escape too often?
Should I have written less should I have
learned small talk or chess?

The sky this summer was dirtier, sky-ier.
كانت السماءُ تلك الليلة أكثر قذارةً وسماءً.

I drove by my old building drunk last week
& shouted Hiiiiiiiiiiiiiii! & welled up

كان الشهرُ شهرَ كانون الثاني
وقرّرنا أن نشتري شجرةَ ميلادٍ صغيرةً متأخّرة
بعشرةِ آلاف ليرةٍ لبنانيّة. في طريقِنا إلى المنزلِ قلتُ إنّي

أفضّلُ نفسيَ الآن على نفسيَ المستقبلية
though I like the me I am now more than the me back then.

Who knew I'd chant the national anthem in the taxi
at dawn? Isn't that the strangest thing?

كاذبةٌ أنا.
تكسرني النهاياتُ وتهجرني الأماكن،

Remember when we read Houseman & as-Sayyab
on your balcony? What was that poem?

وما زلتُ أكره أوراكيَ الثقيلة الممتلئة،
وما زلتُ لا أتوب عن القهوةِ والخريف.

You made tea & I hate tea but that night
I liked the idea of it.

لطالما كانت أرصفة بيروت ممتلئةً
بالهاربين من الموت والواقع.

So you're in Amsterdam now?
Did u buy weed?
We should try lighting up
molokhieh next time u r here.

There are many ways to pretend to recover a city.

يا ليتنا ما زلنا نسكن نفسَ التوقيت
أو نلتقي صباحَ الغد.

I wish we were still in the same time zone.

I think ur probably asleep now
& I gotta start walking to my gate.

لكن لِمَ العجَلة؟

U should c the birds here—
not many of them but feels like many.

سوف أفتحُ بابي ذات يومٍ وأمشي إليها
ولن تكونَ المسافةُ بين القاراتِ متعبةً أو طويلة.

One day I will open my door & walk over,
& the distance between continents won't be tiring, or long.

# We Are Young We Are Beautiful

The square ceiling lights become faint windows
on the clinic floor. The secretary answers the phone,
*Why do you need Valium?*

My friend was summoned & left me
here, holding her cappuccino.
We went dancing last night

though I had a stomachache but she insisted
*Get up get up, we are young we are*
*beautiful.* We sang. We filmed the disco ball the strobes.

The secretary reminds the woman on the line
to pick up her meds on Monday. *Don't be late*
*there's a small supply.* I breathe in, the hollow flowers

of the white wooden door weave in the sunlight,
the cappuccino's getting cold. The brochures invite,
*Heard of multiple sclerosis? It's time you did.*

My friend dreamed of a shadow who asked her
if she wanted to be healed.
She told us last night in the car then hoped

the music in the club was good. *It better*
*be good*, she warned. The secretary repeats *Sorry*
*no more appointments today.*

The evacuation plan on the wall specifies:
*3. Contain: Close all doors behind you.*
My friend answered *Yes, I want to be healed.*

The waiting room smells like strawberry chewing gum.
The brochure explains *Autoimmune means response*
*against self.* Even in the dream, the miracle came

with a condition, as miracles do: *To take away*
*six years from someone else.* My friend
refused. *No.* At the club I searched

for the toilets & she pointed,
*Over there, here, I'll hold your bag*
*are you ok?* I didn't want to drink

but ended up with vodka anyway.
There was blue light & the shadow pulled her
by the arm that often goes numb. *Is this a good*

*omen?* Some days you wake up not sleeping,
some days you don't. *Being diagnosed*
*as early as possible is very important.*

The secretary staples the papers *tshk tshk,*
the nurse strokes the tree tattoo on his arm.
As we leave I try not to step

on the squares of light on the floor—
I want something more certain
& less holy, for now. We don't close the door behind us.

My friend walks ahead of me
& I ask her to *Hey!* slow down a little.
She turns around: *Let's go sit by the sea*

*I better throw this cappuccino don't you want*
*to reincarnate?* I tell her *No,* & she says
*I hope we come back as sisters.*

# UNBREAKABLE

Of the two of us, I always thought I'd be the one
whose body failed first. I slip the socks onto your feet
& tell you I remembered the phone charger
but forgot my night guard—you might hear me
grind my teeth in my sleep. I wake with pain
in my jaw, describe the breakfast the nurse wheels in
(dried peach, bran flakes, pancakes, coffee)
though I already know you'll choose
pancakes & coffee. I open the curtain & announce

it's a nice day outside. My father once told me
hell isn't fire—Allah peeling the burnt skin,
letting it grow back again. *Hell*, he said,
*is perhaps the soul swimming alone
in a loveless infinite.* After the MRI, the doctor
mentions three brain lesions.
Of the two of us, you're the one who loves
more kindly. Once, you drew a yellow daisy
& wrote UNBREAKABLE. The most alarming
dreams soothe & terrify. The doctor describes
the three daisies on your brain. I'm awake now, & unsure

what it meant to be on the kitchen balcony
in my childhood house. The gardenias were still there,
but the clothesline was empty, as was the school
opposite us, which no longer had walls.
The tree with the purple flowers was gone.
I do not want to be standing here,

next to the car taking you to another
hospital. Before you leave, you say, *My son
needs a red shirt for the school show. Write it down.*
Saying goodbye doesn't always come
with men in white, drumming, chanting
prayer, like those who climbed all the stairs

of the city in Ramadan, to sing away
to the holy month. *Al Wadaa*, we called them,
*The Farewell*. When they knocked
on our door, mom gave them money,
asked me to wave. I was terrified

when the doctor named the disease
& told you one can manage it these days—
there are pills, there is time.
I know we are not young young,
know the body is but a shell—
shoulders throb, hips need oiling
at the hinges, hair whitens—
but isn't it too early? & death,
whichever of us it comes for first,
will it be forgetfulness or remembrance?
Of the two of us, you're the one who believes
more. It matters what we tell ourselves,
so we tell ourselves
*We are here we are here we are here.*

# The Body Fails in a Foreign City

The sick poet peels
fruit, watches the city wake
from the hotel glass.

Street signs say ONLY
ONLY STOP—the tree buds don't,
the garbage bags don't.

The taxi driver
mentions Kerouac to soothe
your grief in his car.

A shadow glimmers
on the sidewalk. A bird turns
its head east & west.

The waitress brings bread,
a whole sourdough loaf, says
*Darling. Sorry. Here.*

The green truck wakes you.
Before you slit the curtain,
you don't predict green.

Though you didn't ask,
the concierge brings ginger tea.
Dawn is cold, but less.

This is another
poem for timely kindness.
Blossom-like. By God.

# 4

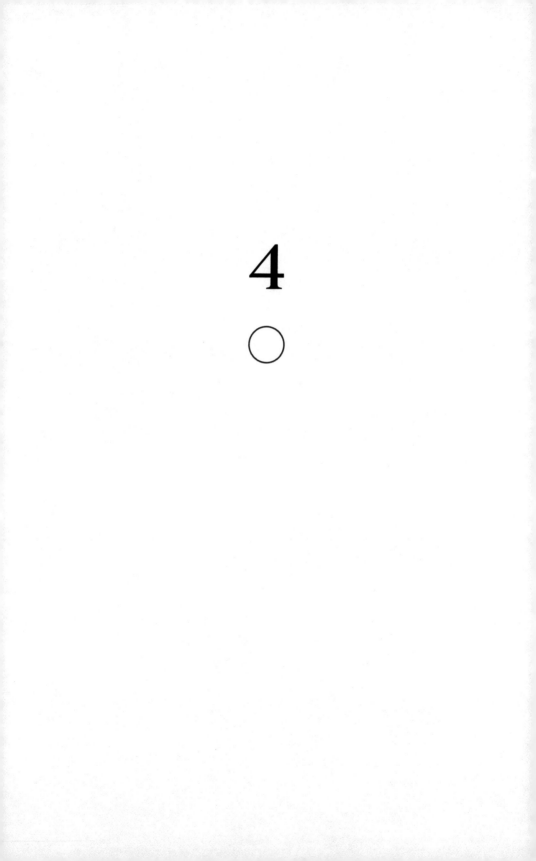

# Fools Rush In

In the you of you the me of me
        a cold sunlit school playground
        a boy in a red sweater chases
        a girl or is caught by her
        I forget which but I remember it was
        beside the football post your smile
        both of us almost inside the net

& beyond that the buses
        the yellow one from which you waved
        slowly lip-synched
        Elvis's "Fools Rush In"
        the blue one that dropped me
        beside that old coffee shop
        called PINKY (the Y fallen from its name)
        where the balding men
        threw dice & rattled prayer beads

O days of mixed tapes
        O copybooks of scribbled songs
        O years of love notes smuggled under classroom tables
        O unplucked eyebrows
        O chipped front tooth

forgive me my forgetfulness
        you looking over his shoulder in class
        explaining something about geometry & angles
        & you blowing her fringe out of her eyes

I still see you I still see you sometimes

        O gentle breath

in the then of then the now of now

# Say Love Say God

I liked the idea of an impossible love.
I was told a love so different can't
make children with souls
worth praying for. But those stories
in the Bible and the Qur'an,
love, we knew what they meant.
When you said *sin*, love, you did not
mean my legs, or the way
you were already inside me.
When you said *sin*, you meant
how one forgets. Do you remember
how we slept naked? You were there.

I believed love is immortal, irrational,
and sometimes tired. The sun, it seems, worships only
the bodies of the young. When I say *old*,
I mean how far we've traveled, love, how we go
back. When I walk new cities, I always
think of you, love. I tell you, *Look—*
*lives upon lives upon lives.*
Sometimes heaven is when I'm away from you, love.
Sometimes heaven is only the two of us. I know you
understand. Only petty loves want to be worshipped.

I liked the idea of an impossible god.
I was told a god so different can't
make children with souls
worth praying for. But those stories
in the Bible and the Qur'an,
god, we knew what they meant.
When you said *sin*, god, you did not
mean my legs, or the way
you were already inside me.
When you said *sin*, you meant

how one forgets. Do you remember
how we slept naked? You were there.

I believed god is immortal, irrational,
and sometimes tired. The sun, it seems, worships only
the bodies of the young. When I say *old*,
I mean how far we've traveled, god, how we go
back. When I walk new cities, I always
think of you, god. I tell you, *Look—*
*lives upon lives upon lives.*
Sometimes heaven is when I'm away from you, god.
Sometimes heaven is only the two of us. I know you
understand. Only petty gods want to be worshipped.

# Ode to My Husband, Who Brings the Music

There are more windows in the new house, so much light
the living room feels weightless. On weekends, I find you
staring out into the garden from the sofa.
You always wake before me, go downstairs & start
playing a song on your phone—sometimes it's new,
more often it's not, & always it works
the memory. When we carved the olive tree near our school,
we could barely see the letters. But after the rain,
they blazed orange. Does bark heal, our names
buried inside it? A name is a wound is a song,
so what you're really doing is calling me. From what
sleep? You warned I eat my days too fast,
or perhaps it was too slow. You once asked,
*What happened?* A balding head, a bank account.
Somewhere, a boy with a black fringe kicks a football & eats figs
straight from the tree. I repeat the story of my fear
of fig trees, how my parents said the wind from the branches
could blind me. *No such thing,* you shrug.
Half of our hometowns thought our marriage was a sin.
A mistake, at least. There were phone calls.
There was hanging up. Years of silence.
& though we weren't a revolution,
we were at least a questioning.
Last week, you almost dialed my old phone number,
& I wondered whether it would ring
in my childhood house, & whether I'd rush to answer.
Only you know & remember the house I drew
over & over again in all my schoolbooks:
house with roof tiles, with chimney,
with lake & swan. Simple, geometric house
I never colored in. But look how resilient
the future is, how I underestimated
the importance of big windows. Of the calm sea
of you. I don't know at what age we learn to dread
happiness. Our first slow dance was in a family club

called Union, in a town too small. We had no flow,
still have none. Unless you consider this—

me in bed, not ready for the morning yet,
& you downstairs, bringing the music.

# when we are we are

the yellow truck behind the city grass
& I am thinking of divorce
the white boat suspended on a paper sea
& I am thinking of divorce
the windows the curtained ones & the bare
& I am thinking of divorce
the utter summer of the summer sky
& I am thinking of divorce
the heat lifting from the asphalt
& I am thinking of divorce
the pink blossoms bursting from the wall
& I am thinking of divorce

how much today there is there is I do not want to leave
how like this morning we are when we are we are
this rupture this rupture

beating with cargo bed with mast
with slow cloud with curtain swoosh
with not yet not yet
beating beating
with the talked and untalked among the cigarettes
with bricks with bursting bougainvillea
with siren with song with sun with soaring with solitude
beating beating
& o my soul my soul
with such satiating stillness

# Ode to Babel

الطَّابق الأرضيّ لمن يؤمن بالحدائق
والطَّابق السّادس للتّسوّق
والطَّابق السّابع للّذين يرمون بأنفسهم.

On every floor, someone waits.

I don't understand what my neighbor asks every morning.
لا أدري ما يسألني جاري كلَّ يوم.

Perhaps: do you have some salt?
Or: would you choose the known or the unknown?

ربّما: أتفضّلين القهوة المرّة؟
أو: هل تعود الأرواح؟

& though I don't understand me either,
I say I am devoted to lemons.

أؤمن بالبحر والموت
لأنّي أجد حبّات رملٍ تحت أظافري كلّ صباح.

The people who look up at airplanes are not from here—

شجرة عائلتي تمتدّ أمامي
أغصاناً مبعثرةً في الضّباب

the metro never moves,
the metro station is full. One day, a man
stepped through the sliding doors & waited,
then another. Then another. Whole families. Etc. etc.

وأمّي لم تجدّل شعري
منذ يومين منذ دهر.

The cars never start.
A blond woman gets in her Mazda every day
to smoke a cigarette, then returns to the tower.

أقصد الطّاولة البعيدة عن النّافذة
في المقهى الدّافئ.
النّادل الوسيم لا يجلب أبداً ما أطلبه
لكنّي لا أعترض.

Once you mispronounce something
you can't pronounce it ever.

يكفيني أنّه يرحّب بي بلغةٍ ما.

It doesn't matter because no one knows
what anyone else is saying.

أشعر بأنّي نسيت أشياءَ كثيرةً
لأنّ حزناً أليفاً يأتيني من ضوء شاشة التّلفاز.

Perhaps we only understand the dialects of rain.
Want beauty? Add water to any landscape.

أحبّ جسدي أحياناً.

I don't love my body. I eat when I thirst,

أدوّن السّطر نفسه ثمّ أمحوه.

& I can't decipher my handwriting.

يكلّمني حبيبي ونغنّي معاً.
تُشيّد حيطانٌ جديدةٌ في المدينة.

No one calls.
Another wall is built in the city.

أنشتُمُ الزّمن الذي جمعنا؟

I look up at the airplanes.

# triptych: reprise

this god of divine textiles
this god of jasmine domes
this god of spray paint
this god waters wounds
this god chants in squares
the dissonant light turns
i hit the wrong notes
of god who declares
this can't be helped

this language of infinite words
for love—هيام is to labyrinth
شغف is what opens hearts
plants grass inside
this language twists my tongue
gracelessly inside my mouth
like a third kiss
all languages confuse me
o who are you stranger

this city of omniscient ads
this city of startling warmth
this city of waste & jacaranda
this city of birth certificates
says my purple palm is proof
still o how i sing i sing
i'm exhausted
all cities kill antigone
with familiar anguish

# Ghazal: In this City

Did we come here to stay, to leave, to escape our wheres in this city?
Autumn is summer, & spring is summer, & summer's a dare in this city.

Dear Lina, I still have balconies. I still have elevators—
they're larger, they silver my reflection. I never take the stairs in this city.

Dear Rana, I love driving on long roads at *maghreb*. See how the skies
fill with birdsong, flame with pink. Sunset's a prayer in this city.

The early trucks on Umm Suqueim. The folded fabrics in Satwa. The workers
on the gravel. The shoppers in the malls. The gallop of the night mare in this city.

Dear Sahar, some early mornings the fog descends, the fog ascends, the fog lifts
the skyscrapers, the fog (part shroud, part bride) thickens the air in this city.

Dear Hind, the windows' watery glimmer hypnotizes me, & the cascades
of bougainvillea on the walls. The tourists wonder what to wear in this city.

We took photos under the bridge. We found envelopes in a minimarket.
We read poetry in cafés to cure our mal de mer in this city.

Dear mama, the peaches are tasteless. I miss exits & get lost on highways. But sand
& leaves circle in small tornadoes on the road. & I laugh & dye my hair in this city.

Dear city, the steam rose from the top of the building & my love said, *Like an engine.*
What propels us? What moors us? Engine or angel, tell me they're in this city.

# Ode to Disappointment

Today, you are determined
to know about the soul. You decide to go
to an afternoon workshop in a bookstore with windows.
At the coffee shop, your daughters play XO
& you explain a diagonal trajectory is also possible.
So many beautiful things go downward,
like your daughters' hair, light bulbs, breasts,
& some plants here, hung from the ceiling.
You realize you don't know the names of plants.
The small one on your table is a cactus,
but what's the one in the corner called, or the leaf
powdered in cacao on your coffee? Is this a sign
of growing old? To contemplate plants & acquire
a love for watermelon juice? To consider piercing your nose
or be seized by the brightness of this spoon, the ceiling lights
inside it like fishing boats? The waitress
is also a photographer & keeps a camera on the side.
She asks the couple in front of you (the guy strokes
his girlfriend's triceps) if she can take their photo.
Your daughter has red velvet cake in her hair,
your husband says he needs to pee. You go home,

answer emails & try to straighten your spine.
Your daughter figures out how to read "exactement,"
but can't tell the difference between 67, "soixante-sept,"
& 77, "soixante-dix-sept." You blame the French. You shout
dictation words across the living room & tell your kids no,
you're not making fries, they should eat salad.
You wonder whether it's wise to start asking them
to like salad when you have an appointment with your soul
in an hour. They agree to cucumber & grilled halloumi.
Before you leave you ask your husband
if you look ok, & he says your hair's too oily.
You run to the shower & tell yourself it's appropriate

to arrive a little late, with clean wet hair & no makeup
to a workshop on the soul. You throw in a wooden bead necklace.
As you walk out, your husband wonders why you insist
on going that late anyway. Don't listen. Get in the car & speed up.
You park & run to the bookstore in the heat.
Here you are, with your wet hair your sweat your
wooden necklace your chipped nail polish, you are here
& the door is locked. The session's been canceled.
All day the day's been telling you this
isn't working, stay home. You never really know

whether God wants you to give up or go on.
On the way back, you call your friend & she doesn't
pick up. You order a latte & the coffee tastes burnt.
You play backgammon with your daughters,
remind them to brush their teeth.
You rarely watch TV, but tonight you flip:
a movie about demigods, a swimsuit contest.
You order french fries & go to bed late.
Your husband walks in, bends down to kiss you,
& noticing a loose thread coming out of your shoelace
on the floor, picks it up. He flicks on a lighter,
& it's not the whole shoe that burns, just the thread.

# Things My Daughters Said

Everybody is a woman.

When I'm older, I'm gonna be older than you.

mom mom mom mom mom mom mom mom.

Is moonlight scary?

I want a pink bone for my birthday.

When I'm a boy, I'll go into the boy's bathroom.

Staying asleep is my hatest brain.

I wanna be a cloud so that I never grow old.

How can I miss you a little when I love you a lot?

Can you call my lost toy and ask her where she is?

Tomorrow is a long time ago.

When I'm a woman, will my grandmothers recognize me?

I don't like it when you speak without words.

Why is the moon following us?

OK can I *laugh* in English then?

I'm the king of all, and of this family too.

If you eat manicure or a lizard, you die.

Do you love me a hundred million?

Teita is a big fan of God.

They're called potato edges, not wedges. Just look at them.

You and dad are NOT married!

I miss seeing cows on the road.

"Terrifying" is not a nice word.

Is God the boss, mom?

I was alive once—it was far away and long ago.

I don't think we really have angels on our shoulders.

# Immortality (or on turning 36)

You say my neck smells like ten years ago
& here we are, students again, drunk
against the wall of our favorite club in the city,
where we danced to French music on Wednesdays,
& Arabic oldies on Fridays, & on Saturdays
it was dark enough & Bon Jovi still
sounded good in "Bed of Roses." My body
believes your hands that travel down, & down
years & years of us, & up to that first
small kiss by the river (I remember
the sound of it, mostly). Will the best songs

always feel like oldies now? & should we
be worried? Dalida has a song where she forgets
she's twice 18 & almost autumn,
wears too much makeup & seduces
a young man. I ask you if, in theory,
an eighteen-year-old god would want
to undress me, & you inhale
through your teeth, begin
to say something when
our little girls call us back
from across these rooms & we walk
down the corridor toward them.

We've become better at this entangling
of our bodies, though we don't recover as fast
from vodka anymore, & the headaches last
longer. Last weekend, we lay hungover
on the sofa all day, & our girls
watched as much TV as they wanted,
& they said, *Thank you thank you.*
We knew better, but still allowed
love to sound easy sometimes.
& yes we've wasted so much, & so many

of our days, but do you remember
your old car? I was jealous of her,
called her Bitch, complained about
the windows that got stuck, & the seats,
but she always got us home, despite
our speed & intoxication, foolish
gods that we were, that we are.

# Ode to Hunger

How I crave the strawberries
we bought on a road
in Cyprus the day we got married.
Their scent was divine & we forgot

to eat them.

# Ghazal: Dear Beirut

*For Beirut, August 4, 2020*

You were never mine. I, never yours.
Isn't that true love's ode, dear Beirut?

I drove friends to the airport, watched them
leave before I left. This wound is old, dear Beirut.

For the heart's laughter, for the eyes' silent
dance, for grief—there's a road, dear Beirut.

The clocks stopped at 6:07. The windows are gone.
From my exile, I click, I read, I implode, dear Beirut.

My daughter kisses the bruise on my skin & says it looks like a country.
Inside us, there's a country where joy is sowed, dear Beirut.

To rage, to swell, to collapse. Like water, you break
in the face of what you erode, dear Beirut.

In my dreams, the sea is gone; the streets, without people or cats.
Then I remember music on your balconies in the cold, dear Beirut.

I carry a name & many cities. They're light & they're heavy.
Tonight & every night, it's you I want to hold, dear Beirut.

# Thank You, Antidepressants

Reader, let me tell you how I keep it together:
friendships & antidepressants.
Long walks on the beach with H
(he pretends these are workouts)
& Nutella in bed with R
(she sends *boil the water you better have chocolate* from her car)
& endless voice notes with L
(she calls them personal podcasts)
& WhatsApp stickers-on-demand from F
(*it is time to MILF* said her sticker with my face
& red lips on my 40th birthday)
& rants with H (another H)
about weight & the lands that spit us out
& talks under midnight bougainvillea with R
(same R) about our mothers' & children's rage
& daily morning phone calls with L
(another L) about nausea & skin & food allergies
she's sure she's got though no doctor can confirm
(& I say *if you're sure you got it*
*then you got it, you got it*)
& jokes across continents with H
(another other H) about impossible geographies
& arguments with M about whether we got married
in 2005 or 2006 (I say our first married summer was a year before
the war, & he says no it was the summer *of* the war,
& we laugh at how we measure time with pain but not without tenderness)
& conversations with G (better name this one: God)
about my dislike for organized religion
& more long voice notes with H
(another other other H) about the opposite of grace.
This happens daily, so thank you, friends,
who are there when the sadness comes,
or when my teeth fall apart
(my teeth do that biyearly)
friends who unscared me

of antidepressants, who reassured me
I won't become another Z or my grandmother.
& yes, thank you, antidepressants,
& you, reader, who stayed with me,
& might be wondering why so many
of my friends' names' first letters are the same,
& the answer is when I said *together*
(in the first line of this poem)
I didn't mean it against fragmentation.

# Morning Prayer

*Sour, Lebanon, August 2018*

Thank you god of coriander & spicy potato
Thank you peeling wooden rails
Thank you god of sea foam
Thank you red buoy bobbing on the water surface
Thank you rock island in the distance
Thank you statue of Our Lady of the Seas
Thank you harbor
Thank you sumac on the tomato placenta
Thank you blackberry jam on the peach flesh
Thank you fumes of the motorbikes
Thank you sombrero on the public beach
Thank you newborn baby in the balcony of your mother's arms
Thank you fat man with the big cross tanning on the plastic chair
Thank you drenched clothes of the clotheslines
Thank you flip-flop girl shouting curses in the alley
Thank you Mary of the small glass shrine
Thank you seagulls
Thank you horizon you are the goddest
Thank you cigarette butts
Thank you broken ship wheel on the seaweed stairs
Thank you full-lipped cashier
Thank you god of silicon & hyaluronic acid
Thank you god of the sun
Thank you god of the bedsheets
Thank you supermarket doorway grandma with the braided hair
Thank you girl behind the phone camera searching for the god angle of your friend's face
Thank you hairs of my husband's beard
Thank you dough of my hips
Thank you old flag in the wind I hello you too
Thank you songs of the colors on the walls on the doors on the shutters
Thank you waves with your ceaseless *sh sh*
Thank you stones of the fortress
What have you seen what have you seen
Little boat little boat goodbye
Little world little world I love you

ZEINA HASHEM BECK is a Lebanese poet and the author of two previous full-length collections of poetry: *Louder than Hearts* (Bauhan Publishing, 2017) and *To Live in Autumn* (The Backwaters Press, 2014), as well as two chapbooks: *3arabi Song* (Rattle, 2016) and *There Was and How Much There Was* (Smith|Doorstop, 2016). Educated in Arabic, English, and French, Hashem Beck has a BA and an MA in English literature from the American University of Beirut. Her poem "Maqam" won *Poetry*'s 2017 Frederick Bock Prize, and her work appeared in *The New York Times*, *Ploughshares*, *Poetry*, and elsewhere. Hashem Beck is the cocreator and cohost, with poet Farah Chamma, of *Maqsouda*, a podcast about Arabic poetry produced by Sowt. After a lifetime in Lebanon and a decade in Dubai, she has recently moved to California.

# PENGUIN POETS

GAROUS ABDOLMALEKIAN
*Lean Against This Late Hour*

PAIGE ACKERSON-KIELY
*Dolefully, A Rampart Stands*

JOHN ASHBERY
*Selected Poems*
*Self-Portrait in a Convex Mirror*

PAUL BEATTY
*Joker, Joker, Deuce*

JOSHUA BENNETT
*Owed*
*The Sobbing School*

TED BERRIGAN
*The Sonnets*

LAUREN BERRY
*The Lifting Dress*

JOE BONOMO
*Installations*

PHILIP BOOTH
*Lifelines: Selected Poems 1950–1999*
*Selves*

JIM CARROLL
*Fear of Dreaming: The Selected Poems*
*Living at the Movies*
*Void of Course*

RIO CORTEZ
*Golden Ax*

ALISON HAWTHORNE DEMING
*Genius Loci*
*Rope*
*Stairway to Heaven*

CARL DENNIS
*Another Reason*
*Callings*
*Earthborn*
*New and Selected Poems 1974–2004*
*Night School*
*Practical Gods*
*Ranking the Wishes*
*Unknown Friends*

DIANE DI PRIMA
*Loba*

STUART DISCHELL
*Backwards Days*
*Dig Safe*

STEPHEN DOBYNS
*Velocities: New and Selected Poems 1966–1992*

EDWARD DORN
*Way More West*

HEID E. ERDRICH
*Little Big Bully*

ROGER FANNING
*The Middle Ages*

ADAM FOULDS
*The Broken Word: An Epic Poem of the British Empire in Kenya, and the Mau Mau Uprising Against It*

CARRIE FOUNTAIN
*Burn Lake*
*Instant Winner*
*The Life*

AMY GERSTLER
*Dearest Creature*
*Ghost Girl*
*Index of Women*
*Medicine*
*Nerve Storm*
*Scattered at Sea*

EUGENE GLORIA
*Drivers at the Short-Time Motel*
*Hoodlum Birds*
*My Favorite Warlord*
*Sightseer in This Killing City*

DEBORA GREGER
*In Darwin's Room*

ZEINA HASHEM BECK
*O*

TERRANCE HAYES
*American Sonnets for My Past and Future Assassin*
*Hip Logic*
*How to Be Drawn*
*Lighthead*
*Wind in a Box*

NATHAN HOKS
*The Narrow Circle*

ROBERT HUNTER
*Sentinel and Other Poems*

MARY KARR
*Viper Rum*

WILLIAM KECKLER
*Sanskrit of the Body*

JACK KEROUAC
*Book of Blues*
*Book of Haikus*
*Book of Sketches*

JOANNA KLINK
*Circadian*
*Excerpts from a Secret Prophecy*
*The Nightfields*
*Raptus*

JOANNE KYGER
*As Ever: Selected Poems*

# PENGUIN POETS

ANN LAUTERBACH
*Hum*
*If in Time:*
  *Selected Poems*
  *1975–2000*
*On a Stair*
*Or to Begin Again*
*Spell*
*Under the Sign*

CORINNE LEE
*Plenty*
*Pyx*

PHILLIS LEVIN
*May Day*
*Mercury*
*Mr. Memory*
  *& Other Poems*

PATRICIA LOCKWOOD
*Motherland Fatherland*
  *Homelandsexuals*

WILLIAM LOGAN
*Rift of Light*

J. MICHAEL MARTINEZ
*Museum of the Americas*

ADRIAN MATEJKA
*The Big Smoke*
*Map to the Stars*
*Mixology*
*Somebody Else Sold*
  *the World*

MICHAEL McCLURE
*Huge Dreams: San Francisco*
  *and Beat Poems*

ROSE McLARNEY
*Forage*
*Its Day Being Gone*

DAVID MELTZER
*David's Copy:*
  *The Selected Poems*
  *of David Meltzer*

TERESA K. MILLER
*Borderline Fortune*

ROBERT MORGAN
*Dark Energy*
*Terroir*

CAROL MUSKE-DUKES
*Blue Rose*
*An Octave Above Thunder:*
  *New and Selected Poems*
*Red Trousseau*
*Twin Cities*

ALICE NOTLEY
*Certain Magical Acts*
*Culture of One*
*The Descent of Alette*
*Disobedience*
*For the Ride*
*In the Pines*
*Mysteries of Small Houses*

WILLIE PERDOMO
*The Crazy Bunch*
*The Essential Hits*
  *of Shorty Bon Bon*

DANIEL POPPICK
*Fear of Description*

LIA PURPURA
*It Shouldn't Have Been*
  *Beautiful*

LAWRENCE RAAB
*The History of Forgetting*

BARBARA RAS
*The Last Skin*
*One Hidden Stuff*

MICHAEL ROBBINS
*Alien vs. Predator*
*The Second Sex*
*Walkman*

PATTIANN ROGERS
*Generations*
*Holy Heathen Rhapsody*
*Quickening Fields*
*Wayfare*

SAM SAX
*Madness*

ROBYN SCHIFF
*A Woman of Property*

WILLIAM STOBB
*Absentia*
*Nervous Systems*

TRYFON TOLIDES
*An Almost Pure Empty*
  *Walking*

VINCENT TORO
*Tertulia*

PAUL TRAN
*All the Flowers Kneeling*

SARAH VAP
*Viability*

ANNE WALDMAN
*Gossamurmur*
*Kill or Cure*
*Manatee/Humanity*
*Trickster Feminism*

JAMES WELCH
*Riding the Earthboy 40*

PHILIP WHALEN
*Overtime: Selected Poems*

PHILLIP B. WILLIAMS
*Mutiny*

ROBERT WRIGLEY
*Anatomy of Melancholy*
  *and Other Poems*
*Beautiful Country*
*Box*
*Earthly Meditations:*
  *New and Selected Poems*
*Lives of the Animals*
*Reign of Snakes*
*The True Account of Myself*
  *as a Bird*

MARK YAKICH
*The Importance of Peeling*
  *Potatoes in Ukraine*
*Spiritual Exercises*
*Unrelated Individuals*
  *Forming a Group Waiting*
  *to Cross*